Burn After Writing

© 2022 Copyright.
All Rights Reserved. The materials in this book may not be reproduced in any way without prior permission from the author.

BURN AFTER WRITING

Belongs to:

Welcome to your book

In The Past

- My first memory ...

- When I was young, I dreamed of ...

- When I look at the past, I miss it the most

- My childhood is described in one word ...

- The posters I grew up on the wall ...

- I will never forget the deepest act of kindness ...

- People in history that I admire ...

My Firsts

- First friend...

- First love...

- First record/CD...

- First foreign holiday...

- First job...

- First car...

- First concert...

- First school...

- First kiss...

- First teacher...

- First alcoholic drink...

- When was the last time you did something for the first time?

Notes

Notes

Looking Back

- The music I loved as a child…

- The first thing I bought with my own money…

- The age at which I became an adult…

- The person who had the greatest impact on my life…

- The person I have loved the most…

- The hardest thing I've ever done…

- If I could do it all over again, I would change…

- The first song I ever remember hearing…

- Things I collected as a child…

- My aspirations as a child…

- The teacher that had the most influence on my life…

- My parents were…

- My first pet…

- My best friend growing up…

- The one thing I regret in the whole world…

- Things that I have been addicted to…

- I was most happy when…

- The book that has had the greatest influence on my life…

- The most dramatic fork in the road in my life…

- I will never forgive…

- The craziest thing I have ever done in my life…

- 5 things I am glad I tried but will never do again…

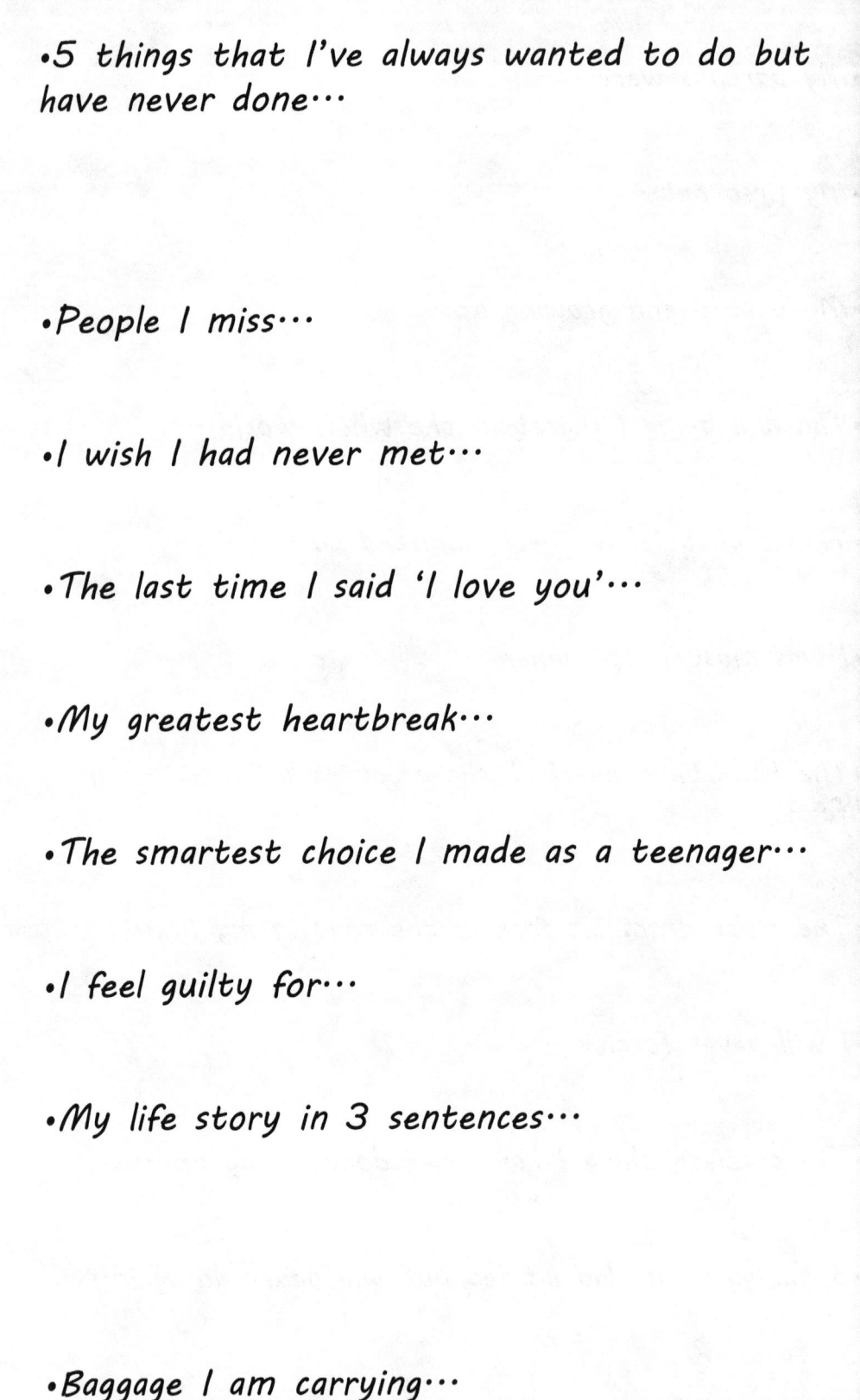

- 5 things that I've always wanted to do but have never done…

- People I miss…

- I wish I had never met…

- The last time I said 'I love you'…

- My greatest heartbreak…

- The smartest choice I made as a teenager…

- I feel guilty for…

- My life story in 3 sentences…

- Baggage I am carrying…

Notes

Notes

A Few of My Favorite Things:

- Top 5 bands...

- Top 5 albums...

- Top 5 concerts...

- Top 5 books...

- Top 5 movies...

- Top 5 songs...

- Top 5 places in the world…

- Top 5 cities…

- Top 5 most amazing experiences…

- Top 5 'regular people'…

- Top 5 celebrities…

- Top 5 creative geniuses…

- If I could spend 48 hours with anyone (living or dead) it would be...

- If I could have lived through any time period, it would have been...

- The last 3 years of my life described in 3 words...

- 5 milestone experiences that made me the person that I am today...

- The hardest choice I have ever had to make...

- The stupidest thing I have ever done...

- How cool would my 16 year old self think I am right now...

- My favourite childhood memory...

Notes

Notes

Firsts And Lasts

The first word I would use to describe myself…

The last time I felt happy…

The first thing I would do if I were in charge of the ountry…

The last thing I think of before I go to sleep…

My first love…

The last time I cried…

The first person I would confide in…

The last person I would rely on…

The first time I had my heart broken…

The last time I said I love you…

The first quality I look for in a person…

- The last time I felt in control...

- The first time I stood my ground...

- The last time I faked it...

- The first person I would call in a crisis...

- The last time I congratulated myself...

- My first real relationship...

- The last time I set my heart on something...

- The first time I lost a loved one...

- The last time I failed at something...

- The first time I thought I'd made it...

- The last time I felt a success...

- The first song that moved me…

- The last time I said thank you…

- The first person I had a crush on…

- The last time I was angry…

- The first thing I would save in a house fire…

- The last time I gave it 100 percent…

- The first time I felt time was running out…

- The last time I was fearful…

- The first time I felt like an adult…

- The last time I did something for the first time…

- The last time I lied…

- Three things I forgive myself for...

- Three signs of hope for the future...

- Three things my alter ego would do differently...

Notes

Notes

The Present

- The biggest inspiration in my life...

- My most prized possession...

- Today I learned...

- Things I should let go of...

- If I was given $10,000, I would spend it on...

- The one song that makes the hairs on the back of my neck stand up...

- 3 things that are getting on my nerves right now...

- If a genie granted me 3 wishes, they would be...

- The first 5 songs that play when I press "shuffle" on my media player...

- The one thing I want to change about myself...

- If I could have a conversation today with one person from history, it would be...

- My life quote...

- The one relationship I would like to fix...

- Things that make me happy...

- My autobiography would be called...

- My favorite "little things" in life...

- If I could give one thing to one person it would be...

- Things that make me laugh...

Notes

Notes

This Is Who I Am

- The thing that I am working on that is BIG...

- My personality in 6 words...

- If I didn't know how old I was, I would think I was...

- If I could choose to stay a certain age forever, It would be...

- If I could go to the fridge right now and find one thing...

- 5 things I need in my life...

- 5 things I want in my life...

- I am...
- I am not...
- I adore...
- I detest...
- I have...
- I have never...
- I like...
- I don't like...
- I love...
- I hate...
- I need...
- I want...
- I can...
- I can't...
- I'm always...
- I'm never...
- I'm afraid of...

- I'm not afraid to…

- I'm pretty good at…

- I'm no good at…

- I want more…

- I want less…

- I can never respect…

- If I could change my first name, I would change it to…

- If I had to be trapped in a TV show, it would be…

- If I could lock one person in a room and torment them for a day, that person would be…

- The one thing I don't mind spending a lot of money on…

- If I had a brainwashing machine, I would use it on…

- The first song to come into my head right now is…

- If I were to win the lottery, this amount would be enough…

- If I could pick up the phone right now and call one person, living or dead, it would be…

Notes

Notes

I Am

Circle which is most like you.

- Anxious or calm

- Stubborn or flexible

- Daring or cautious

- Moody or cheerful

- See big picture or detail oriented

- Competitive or cooperative

- Pessimistic or optimistic

- Patient or hasty

- Suspicious or trusting

Notes

Notes

The Last Word

- Last film…

- Last book…

- Last concert…

- Last time I cried…

- Last song I listened to…

- Last time I was scared…

- Last time I danced…

- Last time I was angry…

- Last time I laughed…

- Last time I was drunk…

- I need to forgive…

- If I could clean up one mess, it would be…

- The one skill I wish I could possess…

- If I was exiled to a foreign land for the rest of my life, I would like it to be…

- My foolproof recipe for mending a broken heart…

- If I had to sacrifice one of my relatives to save the world, it would be…

- The 3 finest meals I have ever produced by my own hand…

- If my house was on fire, the 3 things I would grab are…

Notes

Notes

One Word

Answer all of these prompts with just one word.

- My job...
- My partner...
- My body...
- My love life...
- My sanctuary...
- My fear...
- My childhood...
- My addiction...
- My passion...
- My kryptonite...
- My regret...
- My turn on...
- My turn off...
- My hero...
- My future...
- My fantasy...
- My Achilles' heel...
- My guilt...
- My greatest virtue...
- My vice...

"The outcome is bigger than the sum of it's parts"
(fill in the blanks)

_____ + _____ + _____ = family
_____ + _____ + _____ = love
_____ + _____ + _____ = life

Looking at the lives of my friends, this is who I think has gotten it right…

If I could install 3 complete languages in my brain with zero effort, I would choose…

If I could being one person back from the dead right now, I would be…

The simple biggest waste of energy in my life right now…

People I'd like to punch in the face…

If I could go back in time and witness any historical event, it would be…

The things that are taboo for me, the things I find hard to talk about even with close friends…

- People to be forgiven...

- The things I find ridiculous...

- People that mean something to me...

- If I could make one thing vanish forever, it would be...

- My parents in 5 words...

- The biggest hole in my life was left by...

- If I was given $10,000 today on the condition that I couldn't keep the money for myself, I would...

- Right now, at this moment, the thing I want the most is...

- The one word I would use to describe the relationship with my mother...

- The one word I would use to describe the relationship with my father...

- The advice that has shaped me the most...

- If I could direct the Hollywood movie of my life story, it would be called…

- And this would be the cast list…

- This would be the song for the opening credits…

- This would be the song for the main theme…

- This would be the song for the closing credits…

- Religion in 3 words…

- One word to describe my current love life…

- If I had to sing one karaoke tune in a crowded bar of strangers, my song would be…

- If I were to host a dinner party and I could invite 3 people (dead or alive) as fellow diners, they would be…

- The full names of my children today (born or otherwise)…

- Something that means something…

Notes

Notes

My Attributes

Judge yourself on a scale of 1-10 for each of the following:

Honesty
Generosity
Forgiveness
Happiness
Loyalty
Uniqueness
Humor
Intelligence
Accommodating
Talented
Confidence
Humbleness
Loving
Tolerance
Spontaneity
Health
Creativity
Fashionable

- I'm sick to death of hearing about…

- If no one was watching, I would…

- The most valuable thing I own is…

- My guiltiest pleasure…

- If I could make one thing disappear today, it would be…

- My secret skill…

- The song title that best describes my life…

- If I had two weeks to live, I would…

- The one thing that I do that I would like to be able to stop…

- If I could change one current event in the world, it would be…

- I'm worried about…

- My darkest secret…

Notes

Word Association

Without thinking, write the first word that comes into your head for each of these prompts

Life
Work
Trust
Fame
Forgiveness
Weakness
Death
Discipline
Lies
Sadness
Past
Sex
Excess
Hate
Innocence
Victim
Violence
Regret
Drugs
Religion
Domination
Love
Family
Sacrifice
Age
Honesty
Success
Lust
Fear

- 5 things I love to hate...

- The nicest thing I've ever done that no one knows about...

- At the end of the day, who will be there for me?

- On a scale of 1-10, how happy am I with my life?

  - What would make it a 10?

Notes

My Life In Trivia

Interpret these as you wish!

- *Birthplace…*
- *Siblings…*
- *Currently Residing…*
- *Social Class…*
- *Occupation…*
- *Zodiac Sign…*
- *Political Party…*
- *Allergies…*
- *Pets…*
- *Charity…*
- *Newspaper…*
- *Magazine…*
- *Drink…*
- *Breakfast…*
- *Starter…*
- *Main course…*
- *Dessert…*
- *Restaurant…*
- *Bar…*
- *Club…*
- *Hotel…*
- *Clothing…*
- *Shoes…*
- *Car…*
- *Phone…*
- *Camera…*

- Family is...
- On a scale of 1-10, how in control of my life do I feel right now?
    - What would make it a 10?
- My dream job...
- My favorite food...
- My most treasured possession...
- My perfect Saturday night...
- Something I've wished for repeatedly...
- My hidden talent...
- The things I am really bad at...
- The one movie that I could watch over and over again...

Notes

All Time Favorites

- Song...
- Album...
- Concert...
- Place...
- Movie...
- Book...
- Band...
- Artist...
- Holiday...
- City...
- Teacher...
- Word...
- TV programme...

- The things that money can't buy...

Notes

The Future

- My future in 3 words…

- 3 things I need to let go of…

- I dream of…

- The one thing I'm most excited about…

- The one thing I'm most concerned about…

- My ideal home…

- The risk I would take if I knew I could not fail…

- The one thing that I would be prepared to die for…

- I must make room for…

Notes

This Or That

Circle your favorite from each of the prompts.

The ride or The Destination
The Stones or The Beatles
Mac or PC
Wine or Spirits
Rich or Famous
BMW or Mercedes
Sweet or Salted
Meat or Murder
God or the Big Bang *(just here to point out that the 2 go hand-in-hand very well)*
Pepsi or Coke
London or New York
Nike or Adidas
Tea or Coffee
Gay or Straight *(screams in bisexual)*
Movies or Music
Summer or Winter
Political Left or Right
Truth or Dare

- Spirituality or Religion
- Climate Change Fact or Fiction
- City or Country
- Death Penalty or Life Imprisonment
- Hitchcock or Spielberg
- See the Future or Change the Past
- Las Vegas or Paris
- Art or Science
- Fame or Money
- Brains or Beauty
- Going Out or Staying In
- iPhone or Android
- More Time or More Money
- Subway or McDonalds
- Watch the Movie or Read the Book
- Lennon or McCartney
- Freedom or Security
- Mountains or Beach
- Creativity or Knowledge
- Tattoos or Piercings
- The Wire or The Sopranos
- Money or Looks

- Odd or Even
- Appetizer or Dessert
- Adventure or Relaxation
- Telephone or Text
- Celebrity or Artist
- Cremation or Burial
- Winning is Everything or It's Taking Part that Matters
- How Things Work or How Things Look
- Form or Function
- Thoughts or Emotions
- Slow or Fast
- Optimist or Pessimist
- Realist or Idealist
- Head or Heart

Notes

- Something I think everyone should experience in their lifetime…
- The greatest enemy of the future of mankind…
- My dream reunion…
- If I could go on a trip right now, it would be to…
- The victory I am working toward…
- My next challenge…
- The 3 things that I have been putting off that I need to do…

- The one thing I'll do with my children differently than what my parents did with me…
- The biggest challenge facing the world today…
- The future is *(this can be something that you want/hope for or that you predict)*…

- 10 places I want to go before I die…

- 10 books I want to read…

- My favorite lyrics/poetry…

- In ten years' time, my money is coming from…

- I would like to retire to…

- My perfect road trip…

- The things that scare me about getting old…

- If I could spend the last hours of life with anyone, doing anything, I would…

- If I could be laid to rest anywhere, I would like it to be…

- The one song I would like to be played at my funeral…

- My legacy is…

- 10 songs that are the soundtrack to my life…

Notes

My Pledges

Circle the things that you pledge to do, and add your own.

Say no
Forgive myself for my mistakes
Have no regrets   Priorities
Sleep more   Treat myself
Shake things up   Give more
Fall in love   Take responsibility
Accept criticism   Make art   Be me
Work smarter, not harder   Worry less
Help others   Love more
Embrace change   Listen more
Don't hate   Take chances
Tell the truth   Be assertive
Be more humble
Relax more   Apologize   Lighten up
Eat good food   Smile more
Travel more   Dream big
Feel good anyway   Give credit, take blame   Be thankful

- One week from now, I will···

- One month from now, I will···

- One year from now, I will···

- Ten years from now, I will···

- My 5 rules for life···

Notes

The Bucket List

Cross off what you've done and then add/start your own.

- Donate blood
- Bungee ump
- Go camping
- Climb a mountain
- Plant a tree
- Fly in a helicopter
- Fire a gun
- Go backpacking
- Give to charity
- Go rock climbing
- Learn to juggle
- Write my will
- Milk a cow
- Be part of a flash mob
- Learn a martial art
- Learn first aid
- Learn to fly
- Get a tattoo
- Start a blog
- Join a gym
- Bake a cake
- Run a half marathon
- Do a triathlon
- Ski/snowboard
- Canoe
- Ride a horse
- Learn a new language
- Play a musical instrument
- Sing in a choir
- Dance the salsa
- Ride in a hot air balloon
- Jump out of a plane
- Scuba dive
- White water raft
- Play chess
- Make pottery
- Paint a picture
- Write a short story
- Solve a Rubik's cube
- Volunteer/fundraise
- Start my own business
- Ride a motorbike
- Write a book

- I want less…

- I want more…

- Life is…

- Regret is…

- Success is…

- Children are…

- Death is…

- Happiness is…

- Love is…

- Faith is…

- Work is…

- Money is…

- Peace is…

- Religion is…

- Politics is…

- Imagine you have 9 minutes to live and you have a pen and paper, you can get a message to someone you love. What do you want to pass on?

- My inspiration...

Notes

My Partner:

- The future is...
- Our special moment...
- Our song...
- Our city...
- 5 things I love about you...

- My turn-ons...
- My turn offs...
- One thing I'd change about you...
- My confession...
- 5 things you do that drive me crazy ...

- My perfect date night...
- Where it all started...
- What I love about you...
- I'll love you more if...

- You are (circle):
  - Anxious or Calm
  - Stubborn or Flexible
  - Daring or Cautious
  - Moody or Cheerful
  - See Big Picture or Detail Oriented
  - Competitive or Cooperative
  - Pessimistic or Optimistic
  - Patient or Hasty
  - Suspicious or Trusting

- I would love to learn...
- I would love to go to...
- I would love to try...
- I would love to make...
- I would love to let go of...
- I would love to study...
- I would love to talk to...
- I would love to see...
- I would love to learn to...
- I would love to change...
- I would love to help...
- I would love to stop...
- I would love to be...

- In 10 years time I will:
  - Be driving a…
  - Be focused on…
  - Be celebrating…
  - Be living in…
  - Be working as…
  - Be interested in…
  - Be needing a…
  - Be learning…
  - Be a successful…
  - Be serious about…
  - Be having fun with…
  - Be on the path to…
  - Be still in touch with…
  - Be trying to find…

- Be happy to have left…
- Be mastering…
- Be trying to change…
- Be laughing at…
- Be thankful for…
- Be missing…
- Be traveling to…

- A text I'll never send…

- A memory I'll never share…

- A letter I'd love to send…

- A letter I'd love to receive…

- Why?

- Why not?

- A letter to my future self…

- My plans for the future…

YOU DID IT! You reached the end of 'Burn After Writing'!

Have fun with whatever you do with these! Please let me know, I'd love to see/hear how you used them!

And hope you leave a Positive Feedback
with a 5 stars Review,
I'll Be So Appreciated
Thank you from heart to heart

Printed in the USA
CPSIA information can be obtained
at www.ICGtesting.com
LVHW051249020823
753722LV00017B/1138

9 786599 067990